Written by Nickole Williams

© 2017 Nickole Williams.
All Rights Reserved

Copyright US Library of Congress
No part of this book may be reproduced, stored
In a retrieval system, or transmitted by any means without the
written permission of the author.
Printed in the United States of America

Contact information:
BlakButtaFly1@gmail.com

Dedication

To the many fabrics of Poetry, Quotes, Haikus, Acronyms,
Alliterations, all that will make one think about the many   fabrics and facets of our own Lives. This is dedicated to YOU yes, YOU, in hopes that you will find your fabric too.

Table of Content

1. God is Good
2. Fearless
3. Love, Joy & Peace
4. Quest
5. V for Victory
6. Time
7. A Speck
8. Love Birds
9. Cold Day
10. One
11. The Best
12. Renew
13. Precious Metal
14. Golden Mountain
15. Hot at the Top
16. Broken Chains
17. Peace
18. Serenity Within
19. Wisdom
20. Genius
21. House into a Home
22. The Gift
23. Stand
24. Fly, Birdie, Fly
25. 2+2=4Ever
26. Without it All
27. The Dove
28. After the Storm
29. Hope, Faith & Believe
30. No Bullies Allowed
31. Time Traveler
32. Dare You
33. Unconditional Love
34. P, B & J
35. Summer
36. Peas-n-a-Pod
37. Love
38. Opposites Attract
39. Blind Date
40. Dream

God is Good

God is good, he gives us the time, he gives us the strength, he gives us the mind to use Common Sense…

Fearless

Fear not of fear, fear once the fear has become fearless.

Love, Joy & Peace

LOVING **O**PENLY **V**IRTUOUS **E**VOLUTION

JOINING
ONES
YOUTH

PEOPLE **E**VOLVING **A**S **C**ARING **E**SOTERICALLY

Quest

In the quest to search for love, we find that what was once lost, was buried deep inside, all we had to do was dig it up, only then would we find that which cannot be replaced the makings of Authentic Love.

_V_ for Victory

The **_Villainy_** of the **_Vindictive Victim_** of **_Voices_** with its **_Venomous_** tales full of **_Vibrant_**, makes **_Victorious_** a **_Vendetta_**, so full of **_Vengeance_**.

Time

Quietly time stood

As the rain began to drop

My Heart skipped a beat

A Speck

The Sun blinds my eye

Shining on a summer day

Speck fell out of it

Love Birds

Breezy Summer Day

The sun still shines bright outside

Two lovebirds crying

Cold Day

Snowman melts away

On a blistery cold day

Children are laughing

__One__

Father, Son, Holy Spirit

Almighty Omnipotent

Wonderful is He

The Best

Perfection is hard

Being the best you could be,

Why not strive harder?

Renew

Renewal of the mind

Is like a library book

Senses can become overdue

Precious Metal

In the midst of fire

Burnt beyond recognition

My color turned gold

__Golden Mountain__

The rain caused a rift

Golden corrals began a march

Along the mountain

Hot at the Top

Black or White Mudslide

Choking to catch a breath, can

Get hot at the top

Broken Chains

The unraveling
Jilted historical quilts
Slavery broken

Peace

Peace is knowing that God's love in you, allows you to love free, and loving the me, allows me to be at Peace

Serenity Within

Serenity within, makes you feel you could win. Summer breeze that you feel, and the dreams that become real. Quietness of the night, the awakening of a new rise. The Hellos and Goodbyes, the Laughs and the Cries.
Serenity Within makes the Peace Sigh.

<u>Wisdom</u>

W i s e
I n
S p i r i t u a l
D e p t h s
O f
M a t u r I t y

Genius

Genuinely

Enhanced

Never-ending

Intelligence

Underestimated

Socially

House into a Home

        Habitation
        Of
        Used
        Souls
        Evolving

Into A

        Human
        Overcoming
        Mental
        Emotions

The GIFT

Touching
      Hearts
           Eventually

GODS
Inevitable
Forced
Treasure

STAND

Striving
To
Answer
No
Demons

Fly, BIrdie, Fly

Playing dumb
Is the only way to play your game
I figured out
    We are all, one and the same
No need to cry
    Don't leave no last goodbyes
No need to sigh
    I always knew how to FLY

2 +2 =4Ever

Live   2   Learn

Love   2   Lose

Life   4   Ever

             Goes On

Without it All

What is Life without Living

Losing without Learning

Love without it All

The Dove

Touching **H**earts **E**ndlessly

while,

Diving **O**ver **V**arious **E**ndeavors

After the Storm

A balmy wind with

A gust, I cannot recall

Calm after the storm

Collaboration with Marquell - youngest son

Hope, Faith & Believe

H-elps   **F**-orces
O-ptimistic   **A**-rtistic
P-eople   **I**-ntuitions
E-nhance   **T**-o
             H-eighten

B-rings
 E-nergy
  L-ove
    I-ntelligence
      E-verlasting
       V-ictorious
         E-ndurance

<u>No Bullies Allowed</u>

Love one another,
Strength are in numbers
Stand up for what is right,
Words are stronger than the bite
Educate the awareness,
Be bold in your fearlessness
Stop picking on your sisters and brothers,
and let your inner beauty become uncovered.

Time Traveler

Travel turns time *into a* tremendous task told *by* the teller, tales two-*folded* turned time *back* three-*dimensional*, tainted tombstones turned *over*,
Truth turned the travel *into a* journey *worth*
taking.
The Time Traveler took a tour.

Dare You

Why, Say Why?
When I could reply
I have your best interest in mind
I do not lie
Believe me, you may
I dare you, if you try
Love to stand the Test of Time

Unconditional Love

Unity
Non-controlling
Constructive
Openness
Needingly
Desires,
Inside
Testosterones
Idling,
Overall
Never
Allowing
Lust, but,
 Learning **O**f **V**irtual **E**verlasting,
 Unconditional Love

P, B & J

In between two breads

Peanut Butter and Jelly

Soft and Jiggly

Summer

Hot Day in Summer

Barbecue out on the grill

Go jump in the Pool

Peas-N-A-Pod

You are just like me

I enjoy this just as much

Cuddly as a Cub

Love

Flowers are blooming

The birds outside are chirping

Love is all you need

Opposites Attract

Dog chases the Cat

The Cat chases the Dog Back

Opposites Attract

Blind Date

Boy meets Girl outside

He escorts her to the car

Beautiful Blind Date

Dream

Visions, Dreams, Story

Every Vision is a Dream

Dreams make a Story

AUTHORS BIO

Besides writing, **Nickole Williams,** journeys include Acting, Domestic Violence Activist, Children's Advocate, an Educator, and Mentor, performing and producing various programs, plays and talent shows for the youths. She has appeared in Stage Plays, Cable Access Television Shows, Online Radio Talk Shows and has publications, in the Montclair Newspapers and Grapevine Literature Magazine, Essex County, NJ. Nickole is also a Playwright of "***The Resurrection Story-I Got the Keys***" a Poetic Stage Play and Author of her first book "***A Butterfly Called Rainbow-5 Books of Poetic Healing***". She has since gone on to write "***Depths of Solitude***", "***Love Unspoken***" and "**Quotes & Haikus-Volume 2 -SUNSET**".

www.ingramcontent.com/pod-product-compliance
Lightning Source LLC
LaVergne TN
LVHW051204080426
835508LV00021B/2808